Manage Your Productivity:

A Stress-Free Personal System

to Improve Your Productivity,

Create Effective Habits and

Beat Procrastination

Amber Rich

Table of Contents

Introduction

All successful people are very, very productive. They don't spend time and energy on useless things. They don't have unfinished tasks, hurries, and constant stress. Successful people use productiveness power and they confidently go for success.

Are you happy about your productiveness? Do you want to know how to be more efficient?

Let me share a secret with you.

The answer will be known with a systematic approach. Look closer at successful people. You'll see that they have a carefully-designed system. No method will give a bigger result than a few correctly implemented ones.

The book will give you all the knowledge and tool you need, which will allow you to get closer to the results that you undoubtedly deserve.

Here are a few things that you'll get:

1. You'll know what you need the productiveness for and what influences it;
2. You'll learn how to manage yourself and your life;

3. You'll know about the nature of procrastination;
4. You'll turn actions that help to be more productive into sustainable habits;
5. You'll learn how to plan tasks in a way that will increase your results at least twice;
6. You'll learn how to set clear goals and make right decisions;
7. You'll take control of your stress;
8. You'll be productive instead of just busy;
9. And of course, you'll learn how to make your own productiveness system;
10. And much more.

And now the most important, you'll be able to:

1. Put in order the pending tasks;
2. Rationally use your time;
3. Don't do unnecessary work;
4. Not waste your time and energy;
5. Get rid of deadlines and stress.

And also, as a bonus: once you start thinking and acting like a successful person, you'll be a success magnet.

Thanks for purchasing this book.

I hope my book will bring you not only the benefits but also the pleasure.

Amber Rich

Chapter 1: Why do you need productivity?

Are you happy about how your day went?

Did you do everything you planned?

Did you get closer to your goal or dream?

Are you content with your results and achievements?

And finally: are you productive?

Usually, people who want success are worried about these questions. There are internal and external understandings of success. The internal understanding of success is our feelings, contentment with life, optimism, confidence, joy, positive mood. The external one is our actions, achievements, results, completed tasks.

The balance of these components is needed for a harmonious feeling of success. But the paradox exists in that in most cases productive actions are the ones that determine success and influence in our feelings. Feelings are an indicator that tells you whether you're moving in the right direction or you should stop and change the route.

The main idea of personal productivity is to feel the satisfaction and the sense of success. The more productive you are, the more you feel the joy, the higher your energy is and the more successful you are.

Please note that I'm not talking about the number of tasks you do in a unit of time. This meaning fits better for "production". Also, note that always being busy doesn't mean being productive and this doesn't guarantee success.

Differences of a productive and a busy person

The main difference between a productive and a busy person is the different action algorithms.

Compare:

Busy person	Productive person
Pretends that he's doing something	Engaged in the business
Has multiple priorities	Has a few important
Says "yes" fast	Carefully thinks about his answer
Concentrated on the action	Concentrated on the correctness of the action
Talks a lot about how busy he is	Lets the results talk for themselves
Talks about how little time he has	Invests time only in the most important
Multitasks	Concentrated on one thing
Instantly responds to messages	Responds in the right moment

Wants other people to be busy	Wants others to be effective
Plans to change soon	Constantly changing and developing
Asks the opinion of others	Acts
Uses all the resources	Uses only resources necessary for the result
Evaluates the effectiveness by the finishing of a task	Evaluates the effectiveness by the feedback, which allows consideration of all the pros and cons
Aspires to perfect execution	Avoids perfectionism

What of the above is closer to you?

What tactics do you use mostly?

And what results do you get?

The essential point: applying just a few of behavioral tactics of a successful person is not enough. It's necessary to completely change the system of thoughts and actions. You'll get the effect only in case you treat the illness and not just the symptoms.

You cannot notice specific results of a productive person in a short-term perspective, but in a middle-term and even more, in a long-term perspective, the results will be just stunning. If you don't believe, just check.

Personal productiveness in the context of progress

The need of increasing personal productiveness is largely determined by the requirements of the modern society. And at the same time, the progress creates additional problems for the human that lower the productiveness.

Let's look at common situations we face every day:

The problem of choice

How much time, effort and energy is spent to choose, among all the variety, for example, a cell phone? I remember how I was choosing a laptop a few years ago. It was important to me that it had a number of functions, that it was a determined model and color. Of course, in a few months that model was already outdated and the numerous features of the device were not needed. But I spent so much time and effort as if I was buying the house of my dreams and not the technology to solve simple tasks.

Distraction and interruption

How many times a day do you check your email, watch the news, or react to Facebook posts? Note that you yourself voluntarily distract yourself from the main tasks. Make a simple experiment: measure the time that you uselessly spend on the Internet during a week. For example: "I spent 2 hours looking at pictures when I could write an article for the blog". The results will impress you.

Entertainment

They are many, they are different, and they are available. And, of course, they are funnier than learning a new language or working out a new skill that will bring you closer to the success. Reduce the entertainment to little doses and you'll see how much time and energy are released for truly important things.

Multitasking

We do several tasks at the same time: we make phone calls, we respond to emails, we discuss a project with mates. There are a lot of variants. I'm sure that you know it like no one else. Of course, you are busy and maybe you feel your significance and importance, but are you productive?

Velocity

Progress makes it possible to solve the emerged problems quickly. You can get into any part of the world in a short time, you can find the information you need on the web in just a few minutes, etc. On the other hand, we unconsciously look for such fast personal results: we want to immediately have a nice big house, an expensive car, a stable business. But in reality, we get the opposite, as we forget that the right actions must be done between "I want" and "the result".

I am not encouraging you by any means to refuse the benefits of the civilization. Just look at this process from the other perspective. By understanding the modern context, it will be easier for you to notice and minimize the negative influence of the progress and to rise the productivity.

The above examples suggest thinking about if it's necessary to manage the time efficiently, which means: about time management. Actually, we cannot manage the time. We can only manage ourselves. By managing yourself, you are managing your productiveness and your success.

Managing oneself: increase your productiveness

If you want to be more productive, you must move to a new level of thinking, review your paradigm, and change yourself. Chances are you've heard a thought like: "It's impossible to solve the problems that you face, being in the same level of thinking as when you were creating them". Just realize that you have to change, be ready for the changes, and want changes. You have to change, regardless the external obstacles and internal resistance. Do not be scared of leaving the comfort zone and the possible failures.

The future can be either the continuation of your past or something new that you'll create alone. For the majority of people, the future is the continuation of the past, with the same acts, emotions, knowledge, skills and respectively, the same results. These people don't know how to act in a different way and in most of the cases they don't even want to know how.

If you say "I don't want to live in the past, I'll live with the future that I'm creating alone right now in this moment", this will give an extraordinary boost to your development. YOU and only YOUR actions now are between your past and your future. Take control of your life and say "I choose, I make choices in life, I control". Do you feel your own power?

Develop your talents and your strengths. If you work on the biggest possibilities every day, over time you'll see that you have achieved an impressive success.

Focus your thoughts, attention, and act on what you want to get. Find a big motivation for changes, create the corresponding mood. People who were able to force, control and motivate themselves are the ones who got the biggest success.

Make it a point of support the thesis: every person can be more productive.

The inner attitude is very important, but you remember that specific actions increase productivity and bring success closer. But what you should do if you're constantly choosing not to act, but to procrastinate? The solution resides in understanding the phenomenon of procrastination. We'll talk about it in the next chapter.

Chapter 2: Procrastination

In the previous chapter, we reviewed what does "personal productivity" mean, we understood the difference between a busy and a productive person, we identified what external factors can affect our efficiency negatively. In this chapter, we'll review the factors that have an impact on personal productivity and that depend solely on us.

We'll be talking about procrastination, ineffective habits, inability to plan and make decisions and, of course, about stress. Our task is to learn to recognize and understand their nature and minimize the impact.

Procrastination is a tendency to put off tasks for later, despite the negative consequences. People talk more and more about the phenomenon of procrastination in the last years.

According to scientists, about 20% of the adult population are constantly faced with this phenomenon. Recent studies have shown that procrastination has nothing to do with laziness.

A lazy person just doesn't want to do anything and, what's more interesting, he's not worried about it. A person affected by procrastination recognizes the importance of the actions, he gets ready, plans, but he can't start. At the same time the person experiences true mental anguish: he blames himself, he criticizes himself and he feels uncertainty. The self-esteem of this person rapidly goes down. Procrastination takes strength and energy. The less energy we have left, the more likely that a task will be delayed indefinitely.

Scientists came to the conclusion that procrastination is associated with a disturbance of motivation, volitional, and emotional areas. The hard part is that there are two systems fighting against each other in our brain: *limbic* and *prefrontal cortex*.

The limbic system is an ancient system associated with the instincts of self-preservation and it's responsible for the formation of emotions, motivation, and behavioral reactions. The center of pleasure is also located in the limbic system.

The prefrontal cortex of the brain is a relatively young part of the brain, which is responsible for the will, dedication, planning and decision-making.

Scientists have determined that the personal productivity is reduced when the signals that come from the prefrontal cortex weaken and the emotional commands of the limbic system get more intense. In such situation, it's hard to control our decisions and work effectively.

According to this theory, procrastination appears when the limbic system understands the given task as extremely hard (it interprets it as a life-threatening). Accordingly, it tries to prevent excessive tension and release of the stress hormone called "cortisol".

Therefore, don't be surprised of you can't make yourself start to prepare for a hard project that you have to finish for the next week. Instead of useful actions you go to drink coffee, watch Facebook posts, spend time with your friends. Even from such a pastime, you don't feel particularly happy and the hormone called "dopamine" does not get increased; for the limbic system it's important that you avoid stress.

The prefrontal cortex has a hard time fighting against the limbic system. There's a kind of a fight between "I want" (short-term pleasure) and "I need" (long-term perspective).

Reasons for procrastination

The process of procrastinating usually happens automatically and it's often unnoticed. At the same time, there's tension at the thought of an unfinished or not-started task. If you can keep track of the signs that starts your procrastination, you will have all the chances to tame it for sure.

 Here are the most common reasons for procrastination:

1. *Lack of a clear goal*. It's hard to force yourself to do something if you don't understand why you need it.
2. *The task is too big and incomprehensible*. Because of this, it seems terrible and unachievable.
3. *The task is not interesting* and doesn't have any significant value.

4. ***There are no serious deadlines***. This means that you can relax and postpone things.
5. ***It's not the perfect moment to perform a task*** (there's no ideal mood or ideal knowledge). Typically, the desired moment never comes.
6. ***Perfectionism*** makes us postpone actions because we don't feel like we have the energy to make everything ideal.
7. ***Multitasking*** divides resources for the small tasks that don't lead to the achievement of our tasks.
8. ***Depressive state*** steals energy and desire to do anything.
9. The global problem is ***fear***. We are scared to:

  ➢ *not get the desirable result;*
  ➢ *seem unprofessional;*
  ➢ *feel that other people won't appreciate our job;*
  ➢ *end up wasting our time;*
  ➢ *not finish the started thing, etc.*

Analyze your actions: how many and which of the to-do things are you always setting aside and what do you feel in that moment? What do you do instead? Which negative consequences can this have for you?

The answer to these questions will help you to realize the scope of your procrastination and understand the reasons of its origin. If it's hard for you to do it alone, ask the people you know to help you. It's perfectly visible from the outside.

How to cheat procrastination?

Considering the features of procrastination, you should fight it by convincing the limbic system that the task you have to do is not dangerous or terrible, and it's even interesting and you have the desire to do it, and there's no desire to avoid it. In other words, your desire has to be higher than the resistance.

The algorithm of actions is simple:

you either increase the desire or reduce the resistance.

Let's look at some methods of managing procrastination. To make sure the process went successfully, start by determining the cause. By knowing the cause, you'll be able to eliminate the disease and not just fight against the symptoms.

There are examples below that contain the causes of the postponement and the possible ways to solve it.

Example № 1 The reason for procrastination – *no clear goals.*

What to do: **give a clear meaning:**

1. Identify the most important task.
2. Clearly, define the goal and motivation (What? Why?)
3. Find a personal reason if you think that the task is meaningless.
4. Divide the task into smaller parts.
5. Set deadlines.
6. Immediately start working.

This method requires awareness (in this case, it's an opportunity to realize that you procrastinate) and a clear understanding of your priorities.

Example №2 Reason – *lack of energy.*

What to do: **restore the energy:**

- ✓ Do a little restart: go for a walk, drink coffee, take a bath with essential oils, meditate, go to the gym, meet friends or just have a good sleep.

✓ Regulate your daily schedule: complete sleep and rest, optimal physical exercise, switch between mental and physical work.

The main message is: a rested person is able to work much more productively than a tired one. Keep a balance between work and rest.

Example №3 Reason – *lack of control.*

What to do: organize control from the outside, but it's better to learn the skill of self-control.

➢ Control from the outside may come from your manager or a colleague, or ask a loved person. Show your achievements to a friend. Join a group of like-minded people and share your results with them. Along the way it awakens well the spirit of competition.

➢ Plans, checklists, to-do lists, schedules and reminders will help you with your self-control. A little advice: don't complicate your life with hard planning. Think of a flexible system for you, that you will be able to correct if something unexpected happens. Keep your plan in a place where you can see it, and always cross out the finished tasks. This will give you confidence, so you'll know that your day is going effectively. Don't forget to divide the hard tasks into smaller ones, try to avoid multitasking.

By the way, try to apply the **method of structured procrastination**. This method will help to redirect the desire to postpone a task to the action. As a rule, in the beginning of the list, we write in the 1st, 2nd and 3rd place the most important and urgent tasks. Remember how often did you start your day by executing these same tasks? I won't be surprised if you started doing the easier tasks that are at the end of the list (all true procrastinators do this). Your task is to deceive yourself. Write at the top of the list the tasks that you consider not only urgent or important but also hard and actually, you can safely postpone them. This way you'll easily execute other tasks from the list and postpone these ones with a clear conscience.

Example № 4 Reason: *fear to start* (not getting the desired result, fear of being judged, etc.).

What to do: **suppress this fear with the fear of possible consequences:**

> ➢ Tell yourself a detailed story about what can happen and what can be the most terrible consequences if you don't do this task. Imagine all the moments. Be sure to include the humor into this, it will remove the excessive stress and will invigorate you. Imagine all the moments in detail.

For example, you haven't prepared an important report. In the morning, your boss will ask you to come to his office, instead of greeting you. His appearance is clearly unfriendly: his face is pale, his eyes are filled with indignation, he furiously gesticulates and spits saliva. He's furious. He's asking you about the report which he's been waiting for 3 weeks. You understand that the usual explanations won't work now. You stay silent and you feel the cold from the inside: you hear that you've got your salary reduced, you'll no longer have awards and bonuses, and you already have your car in credit and you promised your son a trip to Japan, and to your wife... Maybe you'll even get fired. Your pathetic explanations are interrupted by your boss, he just kicks you out of his office like you're a bad cat. You fall on the floor and your colleagues are laughing loud at you... You cry, you start banging your head against the wall and say: "Why did you not make this report? Just why?"

This is what happens if you do not finish this report today.

The essence of this method is to help the limbic system understand that not doing the task is more dangerous than finding the resources and doing it. The method is excellent, it removes different kinds of barriers, dismisses objections and helps to look at the situation in a new way.

Despite the effectiveness of the method, I don't advise abusing it. Use it only in urgent cases. For every day, it's better to use rituals and good habits, as they help a lot to fight against procrastination and they significantly increase personal productivity.

Chapter 3: Habits and Rituals

Effective habits

Have you ever wondered why you live and work this way and not otherwise? Your achievements are the result of your daily behavior. Simply said, of your habits.

Incidentally, procrastination is a habit too. If you regularly set aside things for later, that means procrastination has become your habit. More precisely, a bad habit.

Analyze your habits. Which of them contribute to your productivity and which ones harm? To understand it, I use a simple criterion:

- *Does this habit bring me to my goal or not?*
- *Does it give the feeling of satisfaction or not?*

According to my personal observations, successful people have similar habits and rituals that help to live a productive day.

Here is a list of effective habits that are present almost in all productive people.

- Morning ritual that energizes the whole day (balanced breakfast, sports, yoga, reading, etc.).
- A planned day with clear objectives and the ability to adhere to its implementation.
- Difficult problems are solved in the part of the day when the personal productivity is higher.
- Work with the e-mail and visiting social sites and the Internet are strictly regulated.
- The balance of work and rest.
- Ability to choose the most important task and focus on it.
- Positive attitude towards life.

Create your system of good habits and rituals. Once you implement one effective habit, you'll be able to feel a positive impact on all areas of your life. Of course, this is not a matter of one day, and you'll have to make an effort, but it's completely real. Stick to the thesis: if you are able to create one habit that doesn't fit you, you'll be able to create another more suitable one. First, you have to know how a habit is created.

How is a habit created?

The first thing to consider is that our brain is an extremely effective mechanism that seeks to save its effort.

It transforms any action which was repeated many times into a habit, be it simple or more difficult: walking, cleaning the house, making the breakfast, checking the email.

The brain needs a signal ("sign"), which runs the habitual actions (physical, emotional, intellectual) and the reward, that reinforces the habit in the brain.

Habit:

SIGN – HABITUAL ACTIONS – REWARD

The desire to receive the award is the key element in the creation of any habit (both good and bad).

The good news: you can learn how to shape that big desire. Think of a pleasant tiredness in the body after swimming or bike riding. Compare it to the feeling of sitting in front of a TV without moving for two days. Agree with me that the difference is significant. Don't you want to feel again this drive, energy, and good mood after a morning run? Or re-experience the sense of pride for your achievements? Teach yourself how to passionately want to feel again that positive moments that will move you forward.

When working through the **bad (ineffective) habits** you have to consider an important point: habits that are fixed in the brain will never disappear over time. As soon as the appropriate signals appear, the habit will start to operate again. It's impossible to destroy a habit, you can only change it by another one.

To manage and create lasting habits you have to learn how to understand the signs and strongly want the reward. And, the most important, you have to establish a new habitual action.

The algorithm to create a *NEW habit*:

understand the sign

CHANGE THE HABITUAL ACTION TO A NEW ONE

get the reward

Let's look at an example that specifically has to do with personal productivity. This situation is familiar to me personally. There was a time when I was checking my email every 10-15 minutes, which was undoubtedly reducing my effectiveness a lot.

I started to wonder: why was I acting like this and not otherwise? What reward am I wanting? The conclusion hit me: my reward is a sense of control over the process. I decided to try to take control with other actions and I started to check my email 3 times a day consciously, at a specified time. It took me a month to make the new habit become natural and not cause resistance.

In order to ingrain a habit, you have to repeat it again and again, creating new neuronal connections.

I advise you to evaluate your possibilities realistically, as not a lot of people are able to introduce several new habits at the same time. Start with one habit that can give you maximum results and work with it until its complete consolidation.

Consider that you'll definitely encounter resistance. It's natural, everybody passes through it. Awareness (understanding of what is happening) and the desire to achieve better results will help you to go through this period of resistance. Remind yourself more often why are you doing this.

A few tips that will help you to cope with inefficient habits:

1. Have the power to see and acknowledge that you have unprofitable habits.
2. Describe in detail and understand their nature.
3. Determine the effects of a bad habit on you and others.
4. Consider how you'll control yourself.
5. Be patient (at least for a month) when introducing a new habit. Move step by step.
6. Fix the positive changes (keep a diary of your success, share with relatives or with a support group).
7. Focus on the positive changes that your new habit will give you.
8. Reward yourself for the achieved results. And, of course, don't forget about penalties if you violated the obligation.
9. Remember: your habits are the reflection of your choices.

Positive rituals (Routines)

In order to increase productivity and save resources you have to develop effective rituals. Figuratively speaking, a ritual is a set of useful actions that will create a single streamlined system to solve problems the best way.

I'm sure that you heard of the morning and evening rituals. They help to avoid the chaos in the morning when you're taking kids to school, and in the evening, they give you the possibility to plan the time the way that after all the household tasks you have half an hour exclusively for yourself. Detailed instructions to perform professional responsibilities are also a kind of rituals. Develop your own effective rituals!

I won't be surprised if some of you will say that rituals make the life boring and monotonous. To some extent, you are right. But if you analyze what you do in the morning, in the evening and at work time, you'll find the same type of actions, meaning "the same ritual". And are they always productive?

In terms of productivity, your rituals should definitely help to use the time and energy efficiently.

1. Think in detail and plan all the elements of the ritual. The more detailed, the better.
2. Imagine how you perfectly perform this ritual.
3. Write down the whole process on paper.
4. Implement the ritual to your life.
5. Analyze, adjust and optimize the ritual.

Here's an example that I used to use when I was working in a department of client support of a big company that sells household appliances. One of my tasks was to call clients every day and get their suggestions for improving the quality of service. This job wasn't bringing me pleasure and, to be honest, sometimes I hated it!

Of course, I was distracted by other tasks and I was consciously or unconsciously putting them off for later. No wonder that my boss wasn't happy and neither was I, because I wanted to have progress in the career. Urgently, I had to take drastic measures.

With full awareness of the importance of this work, I began to organize my ritual. I thought about all the elements that I needed: a phone, a laptop, a pre-prepared list of clients and their contact data, colored pens, fruits, a glass of water, a notepad, a clock and a mental attitude. And also, silence. I had troubles with this last one because the room where I was working was looking like a beehive. Fortunately,

I was able to negotiate with the management and I was given 2 hours in the conference room. It was my small victory.

The next important step: visualization. I imagined how it all happens in an ideal case. I call this process "mental training", the brain gets to know new actions and "links" them with its processes, and, believe me, it will facilitate a lot your entry in the new ritual. As a result, all actions were written in the list in the form of a scheme.

How it looked like:

9.50 – 9.59 – workplace preparation (all that I'll need while working according to my list) and a mental attitude (I myself was a part of it).

10.00 – start of the work. In the process, I would always put a tick in front of customers that I was able to contact. This way I could clearly see that I was really working and, frankly, it inspired me a lot.

10.50 – 10.59 –little break (eat a fruit, drink water), without leaving the work area. I was constantly reminding myself the purpose for which I had to do it.

11.00-12.00 – second block of concentrated work.

After that, my reward was waiting for me: a cup of aromatic herbal tea with dried fruits and nuts.

This ritual wasn't working for me perfectly in the beginning. I had to review and add elements in the process (for example, a 10-minute break for these last ones).

This approach allowed me to do in 2 hours what I could be doing for a couple of days before. My productivity has increased a few times, and with it my self-esteem grew and my stress got reduced. The results amazed me. By the way, my boss was also very pleased. For each case, when I want to get results, I use this approach.

Try to create your own ritual. The main goal is to create a system that will support you and not create friction, interruption, and distractions.

By having developed by yourself one very important habit or ritual and having demonstrated you that this is possible, you'll gain confidence in your abilities and unlimited possibilities when it comes to achieving any goal.

Chapter 4: Plans and Solutions

In the previous chapter, we talked about the importance of positive habits and rituals to increase productivity. In this chapter, we'll talk about the importance of a correctly made action plan and decisions.

Undoubtedly, every day you make an approximate actions plan: sometimes very primitive (shopping list), sometimes more complex (timing, a mix of multiple tasks). Also, every day you make decisions (easy ones and not so). Your actions and future results depend on your decisions. In this chapter, I won't be stopping to talk about the principles of time-management and well-known planning principles.

I propose to look at the planning and decision making in terms of personal productivity. This approach will be more appropriate if you set a goal to succeed in a significant task, you can also apply it even just to go to the store.

How to plan tasks effectively

The more effective the plan, the better the results and, therefore, you are more satisfied with your productivity. The essence of effective planning is in the optimal combination of the necessary resources and the effort to achieve the goal. This means that you have to use the time, energy, knowledge and finances as much as it's necessary for the result. A well-made plan includes several stages.

Goal

The clearer the goal is defined, the easier will it be to get the result. Compare: "Meet a partner" and "Solve the problem with the supplier about the delivering of goods for the next month".

The second option is focused on the result and the first one on the process. In order to be productive, try to pronounce the desired result when formulating the task. This approach allows understanding of whether the desired result will be achieved at the time, written in the plan in the stage of control and also it helps to understand the own effectiveness.

Resources

In order to achieve any goal that you set, you need resources. There are internal and external ones. For example, time, money, skills and talents – they're internal resources and they are usually limited. In my strong opinion, our most valuable resource is time. We can't influence its transience, we can only use it productively.

Remember Parkinson's law: any task takes exactly the amount of time that was given to it. If you take 1 hour to make a task and you work hard, then your goal will be achieved in an hour. It's very important to allocate real time units to solve a specific issue.

External resources are given to us by the environment – objective laws, rules and what surrounds us. We can't control the laws and the rules, we can only analyze them and use the information from them to achieve our goals.

But what we can choose is the circle of friends that will stimulate us to achieve higher goals and develop more.

Your task is to correctly evaluate your strengths and abilities.

Deadlines

Any good plan won't work if you don't set the time limits. The better you imagine the time frame of the tasks the less likely is to put it off for later. Set clear timing, rather than approximate: this will help you to avoid the delay. To do everything on time is a lot easier if you limit the stages of work by the difficulty.

Use the principle of "60:40", which is widely used in time management. It consists in that you have to plan about 60% of your working time. The other 40% leave them for unexpected situations. This allows you to make the working schedule flexible enough, but without losing systematic approach and it reduces the stress loads. Don't forget to allocate time for the basic human needs, such as food and rest.

Control

The control of the implementation of the plan points allows you to evaluate your own efficiency. Once you see which tasks are not realized on a regular basis, what provokes bigger difficulties, you can come to understand the causes of poor performance.

Analyze your tasks for a determined period of time in terms of their effectiveness. This will help you to make the adjustments when planning the tasks later.

Decisions.

Decide for yourself: To be productive or not

Most of the failures and stress situations are a consequence of wrong decisions and the following reaction to them. In order to get success, you have to learn how to make right decisions and stick to them. This a very useful skill not only for business but also for personal matters.

- Have you ever noticed how successful businessmen make decisions?
- Almost instantly. And how do normal people make decisions?
- How many times does the decision change?
- How much time passes until the decision is finally made?
- How many options do they think of?
- And what about the doubts about the correctness of the decision?

These issues are directly related to the problem of choice. The more possibilities you have, the harder is to decide. In academic terms, this phenomenon is called **"paralysis by analysis"**.

Maybe it will seem strange to you, but making a decision and acting or constantly having doubts about the correctness of the choice is also a kind of a habit.

Thinking about all the options and possible consequences requires so much energy, that in the end, we can't choose any of them. We postpone the decision making and at the same time the performing the associated actions with it and... We procrastinate!

A person faces the paralysis of decision making when he:

- is very overloaded with possible options;
- complicates too much a simple decision;
- finds it necessary to choose the "perfect solution" from all the points of view or expects an ideal moment;
- is afraid of making the wrong decision and, therefore, breaks the made decision just to not make a wrong one;

Analyze your actions and state in the moment of decision-making. Understand what's stopping you.

Next, we'll talk about approaches that will help you to make a decision quickly, easy and without doubts.

Delimit the big and the small decisions

I think the difference is obvious: the choice of a life partner and of a phone color deserve a different grade of attention. Approach the problem of choice from the position of: "Does it have an important significance in a long-term perspective?" Ask yourself these questions: "Will my decision be important in 1 month? In 1 year? In 10 years?"

When you start to evaluate your decision from the point of view of their importance, you'll realize that most of the decisions have little impact in your life and only a small portion really have the ability to influence your life.

Refuse the word "perfect" to "very good"

Perfectionism has to do with procrastination. Take as an undeniable postulate: "The ideal doesn't exist". Apply the Pareto Law 80/20: invest 80% of your time to create and execute the project and the other 20% leave it for improvement. A launched project will bring more results than the one that you plan to make ideal and implement in 5 years.

Define your main goals

In the moment of decision making, clearly defined goals act as beacons that guide you to the right path. The logic is simple: pay attention to the decisions that will contribute to the progress of your main goals. By knowing your final goal it's much easier to evaluate the option that can help you to realize it and refuse all what's useless. Your task is to reduce a lot the amount of options for the choice, only leave the most appropriate for you.

Time frame

Set time frames for the decision making or it can turn into eternity. Tell yourself that you have to make the decision within an hour, a day or a little more. You can also give a public promise (friends, family, support groups) to make the decision before the deadline. This will make you commit to making the decision and avoid the unnecessary delays.

Made a decision? Act!

A decision without its implementation has no meaning. Don't allow yourself to doubt, start to act. Know that, in the way of realizing your choice, maybe you'll need to make reasonable changes or improvements.

In fact, every day we make decisions and choices. Especially in the daily activities, we don't think about what will be the results. Everything happens automatically, at the level of habit. It's easier to eat fast food than to cook healthy food. It's easier to drive two blocks by car than to walk. It's easier to go to a job that you don't like, than improving your skills and finding what you'd like. Every little action is your choice and decision that determine your future. It's time to make a decision: to be more productive or not.

Chapter 5: Increase your productivity without stress

I won't be surprised if you decide to be more productive tomorrow and recover the lost time. Undoubtedly, this is a laudable decision. I want to warn you: distribute your energy right.

Approach the creation of the system of your productivity with a cool head, drop the emotions and excessive worries. Let your decisions be conscious and the actions precise and targeted. It will be more useful if your desire for new achievements glows with uniform stable fire and not burns you from excessive stress. Note that the increase in productivity implies an increase of physical, intellectual and emotional load.

Your task is to make sure that it's a useful pressure and not exhausting tension that can be followed by chronic stress.

Follow the below **recommendations** and be sure to take into account your own characteristics, since no one knows you better than you yourself.

1. Consider your biorhythms. Plan the most important tasks at the time when your energy level is increasing. Set aside simple tasks when you lose energy, motivation or you're in a bad mood.

2. This can sound banal, but you need to take care of your regimen (full sleep, proper nutrition, and physical activity).

3. Keep a balance between work and rest. Fatigue impairs critical thinking and have a negative impact in decision-making.

4. Don't expect quick results, tune in to what you'll have to make strong-willed efforts. Move towards your goal step by step, but consistently.

5. Listen to yourself every day. The feeling of satisfaction from the finished work should be your marker in the productivity management.

6. Take breaks. You cannot be maximally concentrated all the time. Switch the attention and use the relaxation practices.

7. Anticipate a plan of minimal actions for days when you don't feel good. Do things that don't require special attention to the process. For me personally, this is an ideal period to clean the email and the laptop from unnecessary information.

8. Don't be afraid to delegate tasks that don't bring you closer to your goal and take your resources. For example, you can hire someone for the general house cleaning, and in the free time you can meet a customer and sign a promising contract.

9. Don't spend too much time on failures. See them as a process to gain experience. Next time, the experience will help to achieve success.

10. Reward yourself even for small achievements. This will motivate you to finish the task with success and move forward.

Consider increasing your productivity, not only as a way to achieve your goals but also as a complete system that will improve all areas of your life.

Conclusions

In this book, we've reviewed the main moments, how to manage the personal productiveness and what to do to get significant results. Using these principles, you'll be at least twice as productive as you are now. In addition, you'll get a huge pleasure from the process itself. With every new result, the energy level will get higher and you'll be able to get even bigger results.

The goal of this book is to teach you how to create the formula of the personal productiveness, which you will manage. The success of this formula consists in that it combines the elements and creates an effective system.

It's important to remember that any system must work for something; there always have to be goals, tasks, functions and results. The more precise and understandable the system is structed, the better it works. With no system chaos comes.

Before building your productiveness system, answer an important question: what do YOU need it FOR?

What is the goal and what result do you want to have? This is the foundation that will guide your actions.

The elements of productiveness are included in two big units. Let's remind what they include and what you must focus on.

1. Unit "Me and my understanding of the world". In this unit, the main elements are: your thinking, aspire of changes, focus, motivation and, of course, energy.

    a) Take control of your life. Only you are the cause and the consequence of the events in your life. Your results are your responsibility.

    b) Manage yourself, even if it's not easy. Constantly remind yourself what are you doing it for. Don't wait for instant results.

    c) Develop your talents and strengths. Constantly aspire to development. Gradually your thinking system will change.

    d) Raise the level of your energy.

    e) Keep focus and concentrate on important tasks.

2. Unit "My actions". The title of the unit speaks for itself. The main idea: act from the position of a productive person.

a) Determine the cause of your procrastination and find a way to manage it. Minimize the factors that distract you.
b) Approach the task achieving from the position of a productive person. Ask yourself: "Am I acting like a productive person or like a busy one right now?"
c) Minimize the influence of habits that decrease your productivity. Gradually implement good habits in your life.
d) Plan your actions, analyze and control them.
e) Take the right decisions.
f) Organize tasks in a way to minimize the stress.

These are the main components that help to increase the productiveness. Of course, this scheme cannot be ideal and fit to absolutely everyone. You can adapt this system to yourself, furthermore, I advise you to do it by all means. In any case, with a regular practice and a systemic approach the results will be great.

Remember: any person can become more productive. And there's no magic in it: only your actions.

www.ingramcontent.com/pod-product-compliance
Lightning Source LLC
Chambersburg PA
CBHW070225290526
45789CB00004B/1518